THE SUBVERSIVE POWER OF LOVE

The Vision of Henriette Delille

M. SHAWN COPELAND

2007 Madeleva Lecture
in Spirituality

PAULIST PRESS
New York/Mahwah, New Jersey

The Scripture quotations contained herein are from the New Revised Standard Version Copyright © 1989 by the Division of Christian Education of the National Council of the Churches of Christ in the United States of America. Used by permission. All rights reserved.

The photograph of Henriette Delille is reprinted with the permission of the Congregation of the Sisters of the Holy Family, New Orleans, LA.

Book and cover design by Lynn Else

Library of Congress Cataloging-in-Publication Data

Copeland, M. Shawn (Mary Shawn)
    The subversive power of love : the vision of Henriette Delille / M. Shawn Copeland.
        p. cm.
    "2007 Madeleva lecture in spirituality."
    Includes bibliographical references (p.   ).
    ISBN 978-0-8091-4489-1 (alk. paper)
    1. Delille, Henriette, 1812–1862. 2. Sisters of the Holy Family (New Orleans, La.)—History. I. Title.
    BX4496.7.Z8C67 2009
    271´.97—dc22
    [B]
                                                            2008035225

Published by Paulist Press
997 Macarthur Boulevard
Mahwah, New Jersey 07430

www.paulistpress.com

Printed and bound in the
United States of America

of Love THE SUBVERSIVE POWER OF LOVE **The Subversive Power of Love** The Subversive Power of Love THE SUBVERSIVE POWER OF LOVE **The Subversive Power of Love** The Subversive Power of Love THE SUBVERSIVE POWER OF LOVE **The Subversive Power of Love** The Subversive Power of Love THE SUBVERSIVE POWER OF LOVE **The Subversive Power of Love** The Subversive Power of Love THE SUBVERSIVE POWER OF LOVE **The Subversive Power of Love** The Subversive Power of Love THE SUBVERSIVE POWER OF LOVE **The Subversive Power of Love** The Subversive Power of Love THE SUBVERSIVE POWER OF LOVE **The Subversive Power of Love** The Subversive Power of Love THE SUBVERSIVE POWER OF LOVE **The Subversive Power of Love** The Subversive Power of Love THE SUBVERSIVE POWER OF LOVE **The Subversive Power of Love** The Subversive Power of Love THE SUBVERSIVE POWER OF LOVE **The Subversive Power of Love** The Subversive Power of Love THE SUBVERSIVE POWER OF LOVE **The Subversive Power of Love** The Subversive Power of Love THE SUBVERSIVE POWER OF LOVE **The Subversive Power of Love** The Subversive Power of Love THE SUBVERSIVE POWER OF LOVE **The Subversive Power of Love** The

to
Sister Sylvia Thibodeaux, SSF,
in honor of her golden jubilee in religious life,
a woman of insight, vision, moral courage, and
spiritual audacity,
a true daughter of Mère Henriette Delille

CONTENTS

Dr. M. Shawn Copeland is associate professor of systematic theology at Boston College, Chestnut Hill, Massachusetts, and adjunct associate professor of systematic theology at the Institute for Black Catholic Studies, Xavier University of Louisiana. She received her doctorate from Boston College. She is the author of more than seventy-five book chapters, articles, and reviews on such topics as theological anthropology, black theology, political theology, embodiment, and womanist theology, and has co-edited with Elisabeth Schüssler Fiorenza issues of Concilium on *Violence against Women* (1994) and *Feminist Theologies in Different Contexts* (1996). Dr. Copeland is the recipient of three honorary degrees as well as the Yves Congar Award for Excellence in Theology (2000) from Barry University, Miami, Florida.

INTRODUCTION

The only extant daguerreotype of the foundress of the Sisters of the Holy Family, taken at some point after 1852, captures an attractive *femme de couleur libre* (a free woman of color or a free black woman, a term used here interchangeably).[1] Henriette Delille adopts a classic pose: back straight, shoulders level, the fingers of the right hand curve and rest against the elevated base of what appears to be the replica of a Greek column, the left arm extends at her side, the fingers slightly bent, the index finger pointed downward. Mère Delille's dress appears formal, resembling a religious habit—a short dark cape with white collar, dark dress, belted at the waist, a rosary around her neck. Her face commands attention. The hair is swept back to reveal a brow high and wide; eyes set apart, chin determined, a poignant near-smile playing on her lips; her gaze self-aware, knowing, direct.

This visual rendering of Henriette Delille suggests a woman of confidence—even if the group of women gathered with her may face an uncertain future. This image looks out at us on the cards distributed by the Sisters of the Holy Family as they pray for and advocate Henriette Delille's canonization, or formal elevation to sainthood, in the Roman Catholic Church.

The choice of Henriette Delille as the subject of the 2007 Madeleva Lecture requires some explanation. While I have known the Sisters of the Holy Family for more than thirty years, my interest in their foundress intensified about three years ago. As the cause for Delille's canonization moved forward, Sister Sylvia Thibodeaux, then Superior General of the congregation, submitted my name to the Most Reverend Alfred C. Hughes, Archbishop of New Orleans, as a potential member of the Theological Commission formed to evaluate Delille's writings and render judgment on their conformity to Roman Catholic teaching on faith and morals. In June 2004, Archbishop Hughes confirmed my appointment.

As a member of the Theological Commission, my work was not burdensome; spiritual writings coming from Henriette Delille's own hand yield a rather meager collection. Certainly, the absence of sources raises difficulties, since what can be said must be inferential and tentative. Yet, the mediation of holiness, that is, active cooperation with divine grace, may take intersubjective, symbolic, and practical forms carried forward through the praxis of a person's life.[2] This wider construal allows us to take into account "a religious experience of some intensity," which prompted Delille to a conscious, full, and complete donation of self to God that overflowed in love and service.[3]

The Sisters of the Holy Family were not the first congregation of black vowed women religious prior to emancipation. In 1824 in Bardstown, Kentucky, Belgian-born priest Charles Nerinckx encouraged three young black women to form a religious institute. But when Nerinckx ran afoul of the local clergy and was forced to leave the area, the nascent foundation collapsed.[4]

Roughly five years later, in Baltimore, Maryland, Elizabeth Lange and Marie Madeleine Balas, members of Baltimore's Haitian refugee community, opened a free school in their home. The two women had been contemplating consecrated religious life when they met Sulpician priest Jacques Hector Nicolas Joubert de la Muraille. Joubert was charged with pastoral work among the Haitian people who worshipped in the lower chapel of St. Mary's Seminary in the city. Rosine Boegue and Almeide (Therese) Maxis Duchemin, also Haitians, joined Lange and Balas in their work and shared their aspirations for religious life. Joubert offered invaluable support and direction to these founders of the Oblate Sisters of Providence. Once again, the idea of a religious congregation of black women was met with criticism, but Joubert, unlike Nerinckx, had the support of the Archbishop of Baltimore, James Whitfield.[5]

The ambiguous mix of anomalous cultural custom and social status distinguishes Delille's effort to found a religious congregation for black women from these earlier attempts. On the one hand, like Lange, Balas, Boegue, and Duchemin, Delille was a free woman of color in a slave-holding society. On the other hand, Delille's status in that society bounded her life choices. She was a free woman of color, whose matrilineal roots for four generations were entwined in the custom of *plaçage*; she would have been expected to follow that path.

The thesis argued here may be formulated in this way: chattel slavery in the United States spawned a laissez-faire morality and casual religiosity that shaped the environment in which black bodies were objectified and used, abused and desecrated. The murky social milieu of antebellum New Orleans conspired, in particularly depraved ways, to debase the bodies of black women. At the height of the period of enslavement and increasingly rigid legislation, which circumscribed the fragile freedoms not only of the *gens de couleur libre* but also those of all people of African descent, Henriette Delille laid the foundation for a religious congregation of black women.

In doing this, Delille demonstrated considerable critical consciousness not only in understanding the way her own body was framed and read socially, but in recognizing the way that her body and those of enslaved and free black women were framed and read by others, white and black. Her vision and action reveal a grasp of the sacred (or religious or supernatural) meaning and value of black women's bodies; in that grasp those bodies were reconceptualized and redefined. In founding a religious congregation, Henriette Delille asserted black women as fully capable of chastity, as chaste—as fully capable of possessing, choosing, and disposing of themselves and their own bodies. Her vision challenged commonly held readings of those bodies and not only contravened slavery's vicious stereotypes of black women as impious, promiscuous, and lewd, but constructed an alternative to the nineteenth-century system of plaçage in Louisiana.

The significance of Delille's vision and action cannot be overstated. The system of slavery was deeply entwined with Christianity. From the monarchs of Portugal, who required the baptism of the captured Africans, to pastors and ministers who were reluctant to baptize the enslaved peoples, from the use of the Bible as a tool for sustaining and sanctifying the submission of the enslaved peoples to segregated seating and distribution of Holy Communion, even in Catholic parishes, slavery and Christianity forged a dangerous alliance. Not only did this unholy compact imperil the message of the gospel and risk the lives and souls of the enslaved peoples, it endangered the very soul of Christianity.

Slavery trafficked not only in "human property," but also in pornography—in the fantasy that enslaved and free black women existed for white male use. Seemingly unrestrained by personal or religious morality, many slaveholders and other white men claimed the right to take sexual pleasure where and with whom they could. A system of plaçage or concubinage was practiced in many places in the lower South and New Orleans was (in)famous for it. Plaçage allowed a more or less permanent sexual agreement between a white man of financial substance, often a planter, and a free woman of color. By the European aesthetic standards of the time, les femmes de couleur were beautiful, poised, and refined. Some were well educated, many were astute in the conduct of business, but all were resourceful, particularly with regard to their children, for plaçage could serve as an avenue for their freedom.[6] Children born of these sexual liaisons came to constitute a distinctive social group, les gens de couleur libres, the free people of color. Their mothers bargained sharply with their white fathers for their education, clothing, housing, and inheritance; but more often than not the enforcement of a man's will was controlled by the legitimate heirs, his "white family."[7] The Roman Catholic Church treated plaçage with ambiguity:

while the woman's position "was not considered dishonorable," writes historian Cyprian Davis, "neither was it considered truly sacred, nor well protected by the law."[8] Henriette Delille was born into such an arrangement, but repudiated this way of life. The Sisters of the Holy Family constitute a living testament to her desire to create a household freely drawn and joined together in love of God, friendship, and service to others.

The line of inquiry I set out here focuses on the effect of slavery on the cultural and social deconstruction of black women's bodies and its impact on Christian teaching about being human. In confrontation with social constructions of gender and race, Christian teaching about the human person faltered and the consequences for black women were grave. Black women stand, historian Deborah Gray White observes, "at the crossroads of two of the most well-developed ideologies in America, that regarding women and that regarding [race]."[9] These ideologies converge markedly and concretely in the life of Henriette Delille. Historical reflection on her situation may expand our understanding of the complexity of the lives of enslaved and free black women. Critical theological reflection on her experience and historical situation may deepen our apprehension of the ways in which enslaved and free black women drew strategically on religion to secure their bodies, their freedoms, and their lives. By adverting to the practical and social functions of religion, this essay, neither through argument nor intention, diminishes Delille's response to the grace of her call to a life of consecrated chastity and service. Rather, it draws attention to religious consciousness as a crucial mediation of black personal and communal transformation, to the possibilities of self-transcendence in the midst of the direst circumstances.

This line of inquiry resonates with womanist theology, which emerges in critical reflection on the experience of black women. Here the term *experience* denotes the differentiated range and interconnections of black women's religious, racial, cultural, sexual, legal, and social (i.e., political and economic) experience. What we know of Delille reaffirms the normative subject of womanist theology as an acting moral agent, who, through discernment and prayer, intellectual and moral acumen, resourcefulness and, often, resistance, exercises her essential freedom in order to realize the integrity of her life. Here theological reflection not only uncovers substantive issues in relation to being human, but also contributes to "women shaping theology."[10] In striving for religious coherence, intellectual adequacy, and authentic relevance, such an effort participates in redressing the deformation of God's revelation in black women's bodies.

The purpose and limits of this work permit no comprehensive treatment of the religious, cultural, and social history of Louisiana or, even, of New

Orleans. At the same time, in order to understand Henriette Delille's achievement adequately, we must grasp something of the religious, cultural, and social contexts in which she was born, lived, ministered, and died; thus, the theological claims advanced in the third section call for thick contextual description. In Part I, I give an overview of nineteenth-century New Orleans, which was racially mixed, economically dynamic, drenched in French culture, stratified by Spanish mores, and Catholic. This section also sketches the response of the Roman Catholic Church in the United States to slavery, reviews the provisions of the *Code Noir*, considers the situation of les gens de couleur libres or free people of color, and outlines the life of Henriette Delille relying heavily on the meticulous scholarship of historians Cyprian Davis and Virginia Meacham Gould.

Over the past three decades, slave narratives have become an important resource in understanding slavery from the bottom up.[11] Delille was a free woman of color, but in order to appreciate both the fragility of such social status as well as the severe sexual pressure under which she and other free and enslaved black women lived, Part II considers slavery's deconstruction and desecration of black women's bodies. This section uncovers black women's responses to their situation by attending to women's slave narratives. Careful reading of these documents enlarges the context for understanding Delille and the scope of her vision and action.[12]

Part III presses the heart of the thesis: in the context of chattel slavery and plaçage, which deconstructed and desecrated black bodies, Henriette Delille challenged the dominant white cultural ideology about black women. Through founding a religious community of black women, Delille reconceptualized and redefined black women as chaste and transformed ministry in the Roman Catholic Church of colonial New Orleans.

Delille's early foundation had much in common with the societies of pious laywomen, which first appeared around the end of the seventeenth century and evolved into apostolic religious congregations. Eventually, she and two companions, Juliette Gaudin and Josephine Charles, shared domicile, prayer, simple meals, and plain dress; their principal ministries were the education and catechesis of slaves, children, and young women as well as care of the sick, indigent, and orphans. Delille's vision and action sprang from a personal desire to give herself completely to God. To realize publicly that self-donation, she had to win recognition, acceptance, and support from church and society. That she was able to do so, that she was able to enact a new vision of life, even if tenuously, discloses her embodiment of moral audacity and spiritual courage through the subversive power of love. Thus, this line of inquiry is consistent with a liberative theology of religious life; in fact, Delille's action further delimits religious life, stamps its emancipation from racialization, and affirms the nonracial selectivity of the Holy Spirit.

Finally, let me offer a disclaimer. We shall never know fully what Henriette Delille thought or what her motivations were. Perhaps her vision of a different kind of life was reflexive rather than reflective; perhaps her founding a religious community of free black women was an act of personal survival rather than one of religious, cultural, and social resistance. At best, we can only infer her intentions. At the same time, uncritical celebration of her life risks erasing not only her courage and creativity, but also her entanglement in slaveholding society. My claims are theological and they are my own. I believe that the following elaboration offers an appropriate framework for illuminating her vision and honoring her sanctity.

I.

COLONIAL NEW ORLEANS, CATHOLICISM, AND HENRIETTE DELILLE

Under the direction of Jean-Baptiste Le Moyne de Bienville, the French founded New Orleans in 1718 as *La Nouvelle-Orléans* and named the city for Phillip II, Duke of Orléans and Regent of France. However, well before the arrival of French and Spanish settlers, indigenous peoples, including the Natchez and the Choctaw, resided in the area. Topographically, the site provided natural high ground along the flood-prone banks of the lower Mississippi River and in 1722 it replaced Biloxi as the capital of French Louisiana. According to historian Jerah Johnson, the French colonists were quite diverse—hunters, trappers, traders, laborers, sailors, soldiers, former prisoners, and adventurers seeking "gold and silver mines or rich pearl fisheries or hopeful of enriching themselves."[13]

In 1763, the colony was ceded to the Spanish and remained under their control for nearly forty years. Fire in 1788 and again in 1795 destroyed hundreds of wooden houses in the city. Although the style of building that so distinguishes the French Quarter occurred during Spanish rule, architectural historians have determined that these buildings were designed and built by a group of French Creoles along with a few resident Anglo-Americans.

In spite of nearly forty years of Spanish rule, Johnson concludes, "New Orleans remained a colonial French city. It never became Spanish in a cultural sense, and it would still be a colonial French city when the United States took it over in 1803."[14] Historian Gwendolyn Midlo Hall points out that New Orleans, like other colonial cities in the Americas, was the site of vivid, "intense and often violent contacts among people of varied nations, races, classes, languages, and traditions." And, in New Orleans, she continues, "the African imprint was formidable and constant throughout the eighteenth century. The Europeans in this equation were far from omnipotent."[15]

As the leading city of the lower South in the nineteenth century, New Orleans rivaled New York, Philadelphia, Baltimore, and Charleston in commercial activity, efficiency, and prosperity. That success rested in large measure on trade in black bodies. The first ship carrying captured Africans for sale arrived in Louisiana in 1719, and "over the next dozen years roughly six thousand bound men, women, and children entered the colony through the slave trade."[16] By the time Henriette Delille was born, New Orleans was the site of North America's largest slave market. Even now in the French Quarter, just blocks from the Mississippi River, stands a building bearing faded letters that advertise "Slave Exchange."[17]

The Roman Catholic Church and Slavery

The papal bull *Sicut Dudum* by Eugene IV in 1435 was the first explicit papal condemnation of the slave trade. Four hundred years later, in 1839, Gregory XVI repeated the reproach expressed by six of his predecessors and issued the apostolic letter In *Supremo Apostolatus Fastigio*. Gregory admonished and adjured

> all believers in Christ, of whatsoever condition, that no one hereafter may dare unjustly to molest Indians, Negroes, or other men of this sort; or to spoil them of their goods; or to reduce them to slavery; or to extend help or favour to others who perpetrate such things against them; or to exercise that inhuman trade by which Negroes, as if they were not men, but mere animals, howsoever reduced into slavery, are without any distinction, contrary to the laws of justice and humanity, bought, sold, and doomed sometimes to the most severe and exhausting labors.[18]

The pope forbade any Catholic cleric or layperson to defend, publish, or teach, in public or in private, anything that supported the trade. Two more popes, Pius IX in 1866 and Leo XIII in 1888 and again in 1890, would reiterate official Catholic disapproval.

Papal teaching appealed to the ideal, but Catholic living in the United States, particularly in the South, presented several dilemmas regarding race, sex, and enslavement. Catholics, foreign and native born, North and South, were steeped in European religious devotions and cultural sensibilities and relied upon a theology crafted in Europe's relatively static social order. Southern Catholics sought political and civic acceptance without surrender of religious identity and integrity. But, well before the "high tide of Catholic immigration in the nineteenth century," the church had made a compromise with slavery that left some with uneasy consciences.[19]

"Slavery was the shibboleth of Southern civilization. Acceptance in the Old South," states historian Randall Miller, "meant getting right with slavery."[20] Getting right with slavery included the purchase and ownership of slaves. In the upper and lower South, Catholic slaveholders lived alongside their Protestant planter counterparts. Some Catholic families thrived in the South, owning slaves, achieving great wealth, professional success, and sociopolitical status.[21] Religious orders of women and men owned human property: the Carmelites, Jesuits, and Sulpicians in Maryland; Ursulines, Religious of the Sacred Heart, and Capuchins in Louisiana; the Visitation nuns in Washington, DC; Dominicans, Sisters of Charity, and Sisters of Loretto in Kentucky; the Vincentians in Missouri.[22]

Getting right with slavery also meant defending the rightness of enslavement. With conspicuous exception, the hierarchy failed to challenge the culture and system that legitimated, sustained, and benefited from slavery. Despite papal condemnations, Southern bishops and priests held that slavery, as a social, economic, and legal institution, was morally legitimate as long as the slaveholder's title of ownership was valid and the slave cared for materially and spiritually.[23]

The leading moral theologian of the period was the bishop of Philadelphia, Francis Patrick Kenrick, whose *Theologia Moralis* was used in U.S. seminaries. Kenrick validated the institution of slavery by accenting respect for law. He argued that

> nothing should be attempted against the law, nor anything said or done to free the slaves or to make them bear unwillingly. But the prudence and the charity of the sacred ministers should appear in their effecting that the slaves, imbued with Christian morals, render service to their masters, venerating God, the supreme Master of all.[24]

Bishop John England of South Carolina argued that slavery conformed to Catholic teaching and sacred scripture, and Bishop William Henry Elder of Mississippi sought to meet the pastoral needs of the enslaved people, even as he deemed them inferior to whites. Archbishop John Baptist Purcell of Cincinnati came out against slavery just before the Civil War. But New Orleans Archbishop Jean-Marie Odin not only suspended French-born priest Claude Pascal Maistre when he refused to stop preaching publicly against slavery, but also put the parish he served, St. Rose of Lima, under interdict.[25] Bishops Auguste Martin of Louisiana, Augustin Verot of Florida, and John England of South Carolina each acceded to the institution of slavery on the grounds that neither Jesus Christ nor the church condemned it.[26] Martin considered blacks dependent on whites and went so far as to pronounce slavery to be "the manifest will of God."[27]

The Vatican urged the American bishops, both prior to and after emancipation, to evangelize the enslaved and newly emancipated people, but, for the most part, their pleas fell on deaf ears. To be sure, the hierarchy in the United States was confronted with a complex pastoral situation—the needs of a growing culturally and linguistically diverse immigrant population, lay trusteeism, a shortage of clergy and religious, taxing geographic distances, breakdowns in communication, nativist attacks, and the anti-Catholic sentiments of abolitionists.[28]

The Catholic Church in the United States, especially prior to emancipation, faltered in its responsibility to offer a prophetic gospel witness to slaveholding society and ignored its own teaching regarding the dignity of all human persons and the rights of slaves. The hierarchy relegated the question of slavery to the political sphere and, Miller asserts, "yielded up its social conscience to the status quo and devoted itself to the City of God." And, further, he charged: "Even in New Orleans, where the church possessed the numbers, wealth, and prestige to withstand social and political ostracism...the Catholic establishment tendered no critique of Southern culture."[29]

Code Noir

For approximately forty years, enslavement in French colonial Louisiana was governed by the *Code Noir,* which, based on Roman law, reflected the interweaving of Church and Crown.[30] The Code grew from an edict issued in 1685 by Louis XIV to set policy for colonies in French America. In 1722, the Code underwent at least one revision to further tighten restrictions; it was implemented in Louisiana in 1724.[31]

The *Code Noir* specified the obligations, duties, rights, and regulations circumscribing the lives of enslaved people. Enslaved people were explicitly forbidden the public practice of any religion other than Roman Catholicism and were to be instructed and baptized into the faith. Only Roman Catholics were allowed to exercise direct or indirect authority over enslaved people at the risk of punishment for owners and confiscation of their slaves. French Protestants were not to interfere in any way with the practice of Roman Catholicism even by their slaves "at the risk of exemplary punishment," and Jews were to be expelled from the colonies.[32]

The enslaved people were accorded limited rights. These included the right to abstain from work on Sundays and holy days, to bring complaints against slaveholders who denied them adequate food and clothing and care, and with permission from the master to contract marriages. Children born to enslaved women were deemed slaves despite the condition of their fathers, but families (husbands, wives, and prepubescent children), if held by the same master, were not to be separated by sale. Enslaved people could be whipped and beaten, but not tortured. The punishment for a slave who struck a slaveholder, his wife, or children was death. Enslaved people from different plantations were not allowed to assemble. They could not carry or possess weapons or materials that could be used as weapons, and runaway slaves were severely punished. Enslaved people could not be parties to civil or criminal litigation, could not engage in selling "any type of commodities, even fruit, vegetables, firewood, herbs for cooking and animals either at the market or at individual houses, without a letter or known mark from their masters granting express permission." In old age and infirmity, enslaved people were to be cared for by their masters, and baptized slaves were to be interred in consecrated cemeteries.[33]

When Louisiana was turned over to the Spanish in 1763, their country's legal system took effect. Spanish laws regulating slavery were culled from the thirteenth century *Las Siete Partidas*, compiled by the king of Castile, Alfonso X (Alfonso the Wise). Most significantly the *Siete Partidas* allowed "implementation of *coartación:* the right of slaves to purchase their freedom for a stipulated sum of money agreed upon by their masters or arbitrated in the courts."[34] Despite certain ameliorative features of Spanish law regarding conditions of enslavement, the purchase of freedom entailed a complex legal procedure. With permission from the slaveholder, an enslaved man or woman could hire out for work or take on additional labor in order to raise money either for their own freedom or for that of relatives or friends.[35] In *Incidents in the Life of a Slave Girl*, fugitive slave Harriet Jacobs, writing under the pseudonym Linda Brent, recalls the "perseverance and unwearied industry" of her grandmother, Molly Horniblow, who sought to rescue her three children and two grandchildren from slavery. After several years, Mrs. Horniblow succeeded in rescuing one son, Phillip, paying "eight hundred dollars [for] the precious document that secured his freedom."[36]

Free People of Color

Known as the "Queen City" of the Mississippi, New Orleans gained its reputation for extravagance and sophistication, excess and dissipation in the decades following Andrew Jackson's victory over the British in 1815. Historian Wilma King records that one visitor to a New Orleans market in 1856 reported that she saw "negroes, mulattos, and whites, Spanish, French, Creole, and American, Jews, Chinese, and Indians, all dressed in different costumes and speaking their various languages." And, more than likely, King remarks, it was impossible for her "to determine which person of African descent was enslaved or free."[37]

Historian Virginia Meacham Gould contends that New Orleans "was a city with slaves, *not* a slave city."[38] In other words, New Orleans did not rely on the labor of slaves, but rather on that of les gens de couleur libres or free people of color—women in particular. These descendants of liaisons between European, usually French or Spanish, colonists and enslaved Africans called themselves *Creoles*. The *libres* were "light-skinned and prided themselves on their breeding, (white) heritage," cultural attainments, and status; they intermarried, held themselves apart from dark-skinned free blacks and slaves, and constituted a distinctive caste.[39] However, in the complex religious, political, economic, and social caste setting of colonial New Orleans, the status of libres was precarious. Still, these men and women managed, sold, and acquired real estate and some owned slaves. Since the law required freed persons to leave the state or face enslavement, some libres owned slaves for familial or affective reasons. Relatives or friends purchased slaves in order to secure their freedom and keep their extended family together. But other libres owned slaves for reasons of commerce and profit.[40]

Free men of color took employment as shop-keepers, skilled laborers, morticians, and venders. Free women of color worked as laundresses, cooks, seamstresses, midwives, venders, and prostitutes. Sometimes, free black women operated small businesses such as hairdressing shops, bakeries, coffee houses, and boardinghouses.[41] "During the period from the American Revolution to the Civil War, free women of color occupied a unique place in southern history," writes historian Loren Schweninger. These women, she continues,

> were manumitted in greater numbers than their male counterparts, they represented a larger portion of the free black population, and they controlled a significant percentage of the black wealth. Their freedom came more readily because white men who took slave women as sexual part-

23

ners sometimes provided them with deeds of manumission. As a result, in most communities they outnumbered free men of color.[42]

By the early nineteenth century, les gens de couleur libres emerged as a distinct community and with a distinct identity. Henriette Delille and her family were members of this group.

Henriette Delille: A Biographical Sketch

"Henriette Delille must have been a remarkable woman," although, Davis admits, "we have a limited knowledge of her personality and character."[43] Henriette Delille was born in 1812 and died in November 1862, a few months after the occupation of New Orleans by Union soldiers and a few weeks before President Abraham Lincoln promulgated the Emancipation Proclamation on January 1, 1863. Delille would have been about seventeen years of age when David Walker sewed his abolitionist pamphlet, *Appeal to the Coloured Citizens of the World*, into the coats of black mariners on shore leave in Boston; about twenty-one when Maria Stewart spoke to an interracial and mixed-gender audience at African Masonic Hall in Boston; about twenty-six when Frederick Douglass escaped Maryland slavery; and about twenty-seven when Pope Gregory XVI condemned the slave trade in the apostolic letter *In Supremo Apostolatus Fastigio*.[44]

Delille came to maturity, then, during the fractious national debates regarding the future of enslaved and free blacks—abolition or repatriation to Africa—and the vigorous efforts to "Americanize" Louisiana, which tried to curb status and influence of les gens de couleur libres.

With painstaking effort, Cyprian Davis has reconstructed the genealogy of Henriette Delille's family, which is entwined intimately with Louisiana's origins. Delille's matrilineal line begins with her great, great-grandmother, an enslaved African woman named Nanette. Baptized Marie Ann, Nanette bore at least three, possibly four, children for Claude Joseph Villars Dubreuil. Dubreuil was a wealthy planter, miller, and engineer, who played a major role in establishing the French colony. At his death in 1757, Dubreuil owned more than five hundred slaves, but he made no provision to emancipate Nanette or her children. However, somehow by 1763, when she was, perhaps, over fifty years of age, Nanette gained her freedom from Dubreuil's son and namesake. Determined and resourceful, at the cost of more than two thousand dollars she purchased her daughter, Cécile, as well as her grandchildren, Henriette (Laveau) and Narcisse.[45] "Two decades after they had escaped bondage," writes Gould, "Henriette Delille's great-grandmother and great-aunt could be counted among the most well-to-do property holders in New Orleans."[46] As Davis observes, Delille's extended family had become prosperous and independent within the system of small businesses, real estate ownership, farming, and slave ownership. Their women were well placed, successful, and perhaps fairly attractive. If they were not on the highest rung of the social world of the creoles of color, they were, it would seem, in close proximity to that class.[47]

The grandmother, Henriette Laveau, with whom Delille shares a name, bore eight children in liaisons with white men and in 1786 gave birth to a daughter, Marie Josephe. Like her mother, grandmother, and great-grandmother, Marie Josephe Dias entered into the system of plaçage, giving birth to four children, the youngest of whom was Henriette. Neither baptismal nor legal documents record the name of Henriette's father; however, Davis conjectures that she and her brother Jean Delille may have had the same father, while their sister Cécile was fathered by Juan Bonilla.[48]

Little is known either of Delille's childhood or early education. When she was about sixteen her mother was declared mentally unstable, and it is probable, according to Davis, that she turned to her sister Cécile for emotional and financial support. Scholars maintain that she may have been a pupil at the St. Claude Street School, which was run by Sister Ste. Marthe Fontière, a religious sister of the *Dames Hospitalières*, near Lyon, France.

Sister Ste. Marthe came to Louisiana at the request of Louis William Dubourg, Apostolic Administrator of the Diocese of Louisiana and the Floridas.[49] Her mission was to open a school for young girls of color. Presumably instruction was conducted in the French language; the curriculum included "reading, writing, arithmetic, and geography, and most especially religion. [The students] would have been educated to educate." At some point, Delille may have been an instructor at the school. But, sooner or later she would have been expected "to follow the traditions of her mother and grandmothers"—to form an alliance with a white man of financial means.[50] But keeping an eye on the workings of divine providence, Davis conjectures that at the St. Claude Street School, Henriette Delille may well have "received her initiation into the spiritual life and the first intimation of a religious vocation."[51]

On May 2, 1836, Henriette Delille inscribed a motto or resolution in the opening pages of a spiritual book by the Comtesse de Carcado. This devotional work, *The Soul United to Jesus Christ in the Most Holy Sacrament of the Altar*, first published in 1830, presented a series of meditations and conversations with Christ to be read while attending Mass.[52] This is what Henriette Delille wrote: *"Je crois en Dieu. J'espère en Dieu. J'aime. Je v[eux] vivre et mourir pour Dieu."*[53] The translation: "I believe in God. I hope in God. I love. I wish to live and die for God." When she wrote this, Delille was about twenty-four or twenty-five years of age. Since during this period most Catholic lay-people did not receive the Eucharist daily, both the book and the resolution intimate that Delille may have begun already to live or to desire to live a life of deeper spirituality, prayer, and apostolic works. Juliette Gaudin, a free woman of color born in Cuba in 1808 and four years her senior, joined her in these aspirations.[54] These two women would be devoted friends and collaborators until Delille died.

That same year, Delille drew up in French a document entitled "The Rules and Regulations for the Congregation of the Sisters of the Presentation of the Blessed Virgin Mary." The "spirit of the congregation consists of the union of the members in imitation of the First Christians, of whom the Blessed Virgin after the Ascension, was the mother and model."[55] The aim of the congregation was to care for the sick, assist the poor, and instruct the ignorant.

Although the document refers to the members as "sisters," these were laywomen who did not yet live together, took neither solemn nor simple religious vows of poverty, chastity, and obedience, and often were married with a family. The directives called for the members to assemble, at least once a month, in a church in order to recite psalms or receive instruction in Christian life or listen to spiritual reading. The sisters were to care for those among their number who fell ill, ensure treatment by a physician and/or nurse, and "provide the spiritual solace of the Sacraments." The women were obliged to assist at the funeral of a deceased member and to pray for her. Should she leave children, the congregation was to assume their care, dependent upon sufficient funds. Further, in order to support the works of mercy, each sister was to make an annual offering of at least one dollar as well as a monthly contribution of fifty cents.[56] In apostolic aim, communal commitment, and spiritual orientation, this society of pious women was not unlike that founded by Anglican widow Elizabeth Bailey Seton before she joined the Roman Catholic Church. However, as Davis points out, the society inspired and founded by Delille was "the first female religious society of this sort among the black people of Louisiana."[57]

The evolution from a pious society of devout women to a proto-religious congregation to vowed religious occurred gradually. In 1840, Bishop Antoine Blanc sought approbation from Rome for the group of pious women known as the Sisters of the Presentation. Blanc requested and received a formal document from the Vatican attesting that the group was affiliated to the Congregation *Prima Primariae* of the Annunciation of the Blessed Virgin Mary in the Roman College. Thus, Davis states: "It is in light of this approbation that Henriette and Juliette, and a year later Josephine [Charles], began a more concentrated and focused ministry with the aid of [Père] Étienne Rousselon."[58] The year would have been about 1842 and, according to oral tradition, the Sisters of the Holy Family trace their origin to this year.

Delille, Gaudin, and Charles, also a free woman of color from New Orleans, served frequently as godparents and witnesses for the baptisms and marriages of slaves and people of color.[59] Initially, Rousselon helped the three to acquire a house on St. Bernard Street, but when municipal officials brought a wounded man to them for care, for the sake of propriety, they moved into a small house on Bayou Road. This house, which Davis calls "the cradle" of the fledgling group, was constructed for them and partially financed by the modest inheritance Delille received on the death of her mother.[60]

No horarium or schedule of daily communal life on Bayou Road remains extant, but Delille, Gaudin, and Charles took on the "corporal works of mercy." The women catechized slaves and free people of color, taught basic literacy, sheltered orphans, and nursed the sick, the elderly, and the destitute with food and clothing. By 1851, these three demonstrated sufficient understanding of and readiness for religious life, thus "satisfy[ing] the archdiocese that they might make religious vows."[61] Clark and Gould conclude that by 1852, "the three women changed their dress—from blue to black— began wearing rosaries around their necks and took private vows, committing themselves to the church and to those they called 'our people.'"[62]

In view of this dedication, the involvement of Henriette Delille in slaveholding perplexes. In his study of notarial documents, Davis discovered Delille's name in two transactions of sale regarding enslaved women. In 1835, Delille gave a slave named Polly to her sister Cécile Bonille; in three successive wills drawn up in 1851, 1852, and 1860, she made provision for a slave named Betsy and, in the second and third versions, directed her brother Jean Delille to manumit the woman.[63]

In the latter case, Davis was unable to establish Betsy's identity or the precise circumstances by which Delille came to hold the woman, but legislation regulating manumission may have proved an obstacle in the wills of 1850 and 1851. In 1830, the law required newly emancipated slaves to leave the state of Louisiana within thirty days or be reenslaved; to guarantee the slave's departure, the slaveholder was required to post a $1,000 bond.[64] In 1850, the Fugitive Slave Law abrogated the liberty and rights of runaway slaves and free blacks, putting them at risk of seizure and return or sale to traders and incriminating whites in slave catching.[65] In 1852, Louisiana legislation required that freed slaves go to Liberia or be reenslaved.[66] Such legal restrictions may have posed financial, emotional, and physical hardships both for Betsy and for Delille.

The former case is just as complicated. In a will drawn up in 1823, Samuel Hart, a wealthy New Orleans merchant, stipulated the emancipation of an enslaved woman named Polly and her son John. Hart was the man with whom Cécile Bonille had been *placed* and by whom she bore four children. Prior to his death in 1832, Hart revised his will, omitting mention of the manumission of Polly and John. After his death, the executors of Hart's estate sued Cécile for promissory notes that Hart had given her. They inventoried Hart's possessions for sale and included an enslaved woman named Polly. Davis surmises that, if this is the same Polly, she may have requested to live with Cécile. Since Cécile was embroiled in a legal suit with Hart's white heirs, Henriette and [Antonio] Baptistista may have acted on her behalf.[67]

We cannot know the motives or feelings of either Henriette or Cécile; nor can we know the motives or feelings of Betsy or Polly. We cannot know the "true relationships between these [four] women and the nature of their interactions." Perhaps we may say that Henriette Delille prized human dignity and the integrity of black women's bodies and, in doing so, "jeopardized her own well-being and crossed a boundary designed to separate slaves from free persons."[68]

Henriette Delille died of tuberculosis on November 17, 1862, at the age of fifty. For more than twenty-five years, she had "devoted herself without reserve" to ministering to the souls and bodies of slaves.[69] That ministry shamed the "racially limited parameters of antebellum white benevolence" and exposed the timidity of the church.[70] At the age of twenty-four, Henriette Delille resolved to love, to live, and to die for God, and she had.

II.

THE DECONSTRUCTION AND DESECRATION OF BLACK WOMEN'S BODIES

The body constitutes the most public, the most personal, the most intimate thing that a human being possesses.[71] Slavery deconstructed the black body into parts and by price; it obscured black human subjectivity, reassembled bodies as objects packaged for sale, and desecrated black embodied humanness. As historian Stephanie Camp observes, perceptions of the black body were "central, materially and symbolically, to the formation of slaveholding mastery."[72] White male travelers to the African Continent in the sixteenth and seventeenth centuries depicted African women as savage, crude, shameless, and displaying a "rugged reproductive capacity."[73] Drawing on these representations, slaveholders de-gendered black women and reckoned them naturally fit for drudge labor and breeding even as their pornographic gaze carved a line from commercial profit to sexual fantasy and back again.

Marketing Bodies

The antebellum slave market exposed, displayed, and examined black flesh, turning people into objects for sale, purchase, and use. Slave traders advertised their human merchandise by sex, racial classification, age, and skill. Walter Johnson, an historian of the slave market, found that buyers preferred darker-skinned people for labor in fields, lighter-skinned people for skilled or domestic work. Buyers considered "prime age" for laborers at about fifteen to twenty-five years of age, while skilled workers might reach their prime at thirty-five.[74] Men and women were lined up along opposite walls of slave pens allowing buyers comparison by sex. Traders developed a "detailed racial taxonomy" to calibrate the mixture of "black" and "white"— Negro, Griffe, Mulatto, Quadroons, and Octoroon. Traders and buyers correlated the skin color of slaves with occupation or task and intelligence. For example, light-skinned men were assigned to jobs such as coopers or carpenters or carriage drivers, dark-skinned men to work in the field or smithy. Light-skinned women were assigned to domestic work as maids or nurses, dark-skinned women to the kitchen or the field. This color-coded division of labor was neither fixed nor rigid, but nearly always light skin was associated with intelligence.[75]

Buyers scrutinized bodies for signs of illness or injury or scars from whippings, inspected teeth, and manipulated muscles, joints, and fingers. Solomon Northup, born a free man in the state of New York, was kidnapped into slavery in 1841, and placed on auction in New Orleans. In *Twelve Years a Slave*, Northup recalled how slave trader Theophilous Freeman

> would make us hold up our heads, walk briskly back and forth, while customers would feel of our hands and arms and bodies, turn us about, ask us what we could do, make us open our mouths and show our teeth, precisely as a jockey examines a horse which he is about to barter for purchase.[76]

Slaves were ordered to roll up the legs of pants, to remove coats or shirts, to lift skirts in order that buyers could examine their bodies more closely.

But those bodies also could be disguised, "disciplined into order and decorated for market…packaged for sale."[77] Hired out to Missouri slave trader James Walker, William Wells Brown wrote that he was instructed to shave the grizzled facial hair of men and pull out or darken grey strands to hide age.[78] Slaveholders were literally looking for sound, "likely"[79] bodies, thus predicting not only skill, physical stamina, and prowess, but also the growth and stability of their wealth.

Breeding

While there is scant historical evidence that large numbers of slaveholders took up breeding slaves for market, extant reports are unsettling. Freed woman Fannie Moore told an interviewer that "the 'breeding women' always brought more money" than other slaves at market, even the men.[80] Calvin Smith was said to have kept "fifty to sixty head of women...constantly for breeding" on his plantation yielding "twenty to twenty-five children a year, [who] as soon as they were ready for market, [were] taken away and sold, as mule or other cattle..."[81] Some slaveholders forced or attempted to force female slaves to have sex with designated male slaves against their will. When Rose Williams resisted such an order, slaveholder Hawkins declared, "Woman, I've paid big money for you, and I've done so because I want you to have children."[82] Threatened with being whipped at the stake, Williams acquiesced. Brown reported that slaveholder John Calvert so brutally beat an enslaved woman named Lavinia, when she refused to wed the man he selected for her, that "it would have been the same if she had [died]."[83] Freed woman Julia Brown said that some slaveholders refused to allow slaves to marry those from other plantations, insisting that they take partners from among the people on plantations where they were held.[84] An enslaved woman's capacity to reproduce human capital was crucial to slaveholding, but she was to do so when and as slaveholders commanded.

Sexual Exploitation

Slavery shaped Southern, indeed, the national economy, even as it twisted the mind. The slave market was awash in sexuality and the market's rituals of inspection were titillating with "white men, examining slaves, searching out hidden body parts, running hands over limbs, massaging abdomens and articulating pelvic joints, probing wounds and scars with fingers..."[85] Slavery traded in pornography, in the fantasy that black female bodies existed to satisfy the slaveholder's sexual desire, that her body could be bent and shaped to his appetite. Missouri slave trader James Walker raped his female slave, Cynthia, then, years later sold her and the four children she bore him. John Newsome sexually assaulted fourteen-year-old Celia minutes after leaving the slave market, and within five years she gave birth to his two children. John Hoover, in what may have been an attempt to abort his own child, physically tortured Mira until she died. Austin Miller purchased and raped, immediately impregnating, eleven-year-old Sophie, the future great-great-grandmother of critical legal theorist Patricia J. Williams.[86] Through such abuse of patriarchy and racial privilege, these men spewed their moral obscenity, sadism, and force on black female bodies.

Elizabeth Sparks alluded to her master's sexual activity: "Old Master did so much wrong. I couldn't tell you all of it. Slave girl Betty Lilly always had good clothes and all the privileges. She was a favorite of his. But I can't tell all [I know. But] God knows all."[87] On the other hand, Mary Reynolds discussed her master's sexual practices frankly: "We knew that [Dr. Kilpatrick] took a black woman quick as he did a white and took any on his place he wanted, and he took them often." [88]

Held in a slave pen in the nation's capital, Northup recalled an encounter with an enslaved woman whose dress, comportment, and diction intimated that she once had "stood above the common level." Eliza had been owned by Elisha Berry, who pledged to emancipate her and her children, if she would live with him as his mistress. The woman bore at least one child by Berry, a daughter, Emily, whom Northup described as about "seven or eight years old, of light complexion, and with a face of admirable beauty...her hair [falling] in curls around her neck." After some years, Berry lost control of his estate and Eliza and Emily came into the possession of Berry's son-in-law, Jacob Brooks. Brooks contrived to dispose of the pair, who had become objects of his wife's and mother-in-law's ire. Brought to the city under the pretense of securing papers of manumission, the enslaved woman and her child were turned over to a trader, who shipped them to New Orleans.[89]

When Eliza pleaded with the man who had purchased her to bid for her daughter as well, Northup says that trader Freeman rebuffed the man's inquiry:

> There were heaps and piles of money to be made on [Emily], he said, when she was a few years older. There were men enough in New Orleans who would give five thousand dollars for such an extra, handsome, fancy piece as Emily would be, rather than not get her. No, no, he would not sell her then. She was a beauty—a picture—a doll...[90]

Elisha Berry coerced Eliza into sexual relations, and she wagered her body for the sake of freedom—her own and that of her children. But her daughter's body, tagged as a "fancy piece [became] a slaveholder's desire made material in the shape of a little girl."[91] It is not surprising that enslaved women feared the sexual exploitation and degradation of their daughters. Upon learning that her second child was female, Harriet Jacobs said that her "heart was heavier than it had ever been before." She was discreet if urgent in her criticism: "Slavery is terrible for men but it is far more terrible for women. Superceded to the burden common to all *they* have wrongs, and sufferings, and mortifications peculiarly their own."[92]

Jacobs's anxiety sprang from personal experience in the Flint household, which she called a "cage of obscene birds."[93] From the age of fifteen, she was assaulted almost daily by the lewd comments and notes of slaveholder Dr. Flint. Jacobs resisted his advances but, perceiving neither escape nor relief, took a white lover, Mr. Sands. She assumed that her pregnancy would so enrage Flint that he would sell her to her lover. She hoped that Sands would protect her and their children, since custom dictated that the legal status of the child followed that of the mother. Flint rejected Sands's offer and took every opportunity to remind Jacobs that her children added to his "stock of slaves" and would bring "a handsome sum of money" at market.[94]

A few slaveholders flaunted their relations with black women. Johnson singles out New Orleans newspaper editor John Powell, who "entertained his dinner guests at a house inhabited by his 'Quadroon mistress' and the couple's child."[95] Other slaveholders concealed their sexual activity with enslaved women. Yet, whether dissuaded by putative conventions of propriety or the arrogance of indifference, few white people connected to the slave trade spoke publicly about sex between slaveholding white men and enslaved black women. Jacobs commented on this conspiracy of silence and the tacit knowledge it covered:

My master [Dr. Flint] was, to my knowledge, the father of eleven slaves. But did the mothers dare to tell who was the father of their children? Did the other slaves dare to allude to it, except in whispers among themselves? No, indeed. They knew too well the terrible consequences.[96]

Slaveholder Mary Boykin Chestnut confided to her diary, "Any lady is ready to tell you who is the father of all the mulatto children in everybody's household but her own. Those she seems to think, drop from the clouds."[97] Freed woman Savilla Burrell said that her master (Captain Tom Still) fathered children by women enslaved on his plantation. But the gossip of Still's neighbors distressed his wife, prompting Still to sell the children to a trader.[98]

The enslaved people on the Kilpatrick plantation took notice of Margaret, a young light-skinned woman that the doctor brought from Baton Rouge to work as a seamstress. They also took notice of the house that he built for her and set apart from both the slave quarter and the "big house." The fair-skinned children she rapidly bore Kilpatrick testified to her fecundity. On one occasion, Kilpatrick's wife overheard Margaret's children claiming that Kilpatrick "is our daddy [too, and] comes to see us nearly every day and brings us clothes and things from town." That evening, Reynolds said, a furious Mrs. Kilpatrick met her husband with steely silence and refusal of conjugal relations.[99]

The treatment and condition of black women during slavocracy generate a commentary on the underside of morality. The bodies of black women were used as a playing ground on which white male slaveholders, their sons, and slave traders sowed aggressive sexual spite. These same men demanded that white women exemplify sexual propriety, marital fidelity, and devoted motherhood. White women held ambiguous status under slaveholding patriarchy: Nearly all married white women relinquished control over their finances and real estate (including their "human property") to their husbands and were subject to their decisions. The cultural mores of the "cult of true womanhood" checked them at every turn. According to feminist historian Barbara Welter, white women were judged by their husbands, families, neighbors, and the larger society by their adherence to "four cardinal virtues—piety, purity, submissiveness and domesticity...With them she was promised happiness and power."[100] Many white women judged themselves by these standards and acquiesced, giving birth to heirs to human property and embracing what racial privilege and power they could. Shamed at the memory of Flint's sexual harassment and her own sexual defiance, Jacobs asserted, "that which commands admiration in the white woman only hastens the degradation of the female slave."[101]

The "technology" of the slave market reduced black women's bodies to parts for use and abuse and, as womanist theologian Delores Williams has shown, coerced them into surrogacy at every level—substituting as crop hands in fields, laborers on road gangs, wet nurses, maids of all work, objects of sexual release, tools of reproductive capital.[102] But that technology not only made black bodies physically and sexually vulnerable, it came close to "soul murder,"[103] cornering black women in an untenable situation. Commodified, fungible, and labeled as lascivious, black women were made something less than human, but *not* persons.[104] "Soul murder" defines the psychic alienation of enslaved women (and men) from themselves—their bodies, feeling, and memories; it battered the will to resist. This murder survives in the insidious trans-generational black disdain and contempt for the black body, the black other, the black self.[105] The conditions for the possibility of this murder materialized in the collusion of Christianity with the cultural mores and sociopolitical power of slavocracy.

Christianity and the Black Body

Slavery made a charade of religion and co-opted the Christian churches, which offered only limited serious pastoral and theological resistance and little defense of the humanity of the enslaved people. Protestant ministers and pastors conformed to the expectations of the slaveholding elite. They bent doctrine to white cultural supremacy and sanctified the enslavement of black human beings as divinely ordered and, therefore, natural.[106] Given a theology and pastoral perspective forged in the "old world," Catholics found the Protestant South difficult to navigate. But foreign-born and American-born Catholics—clerics, vowed religious, and laity—engaged in slaveholding and provided no strenuous critique of the morals and customs of slavocracy. Jesuit Brother Joseph Mobberly, overseer on the rural Maryland plantation owned by the order, advocated the obligation of slaveholders to prepare slaves for the sacraments. But Miller remarks, "[Mobberly] did not do very well with his [own] black wards."[107] Jacobs skewered the behavior of a town constable and Methodist class leader, "who bought and sold slaves, who whipped his brethren and sisters of the church at the public whipping post, in jail or out of jail."[108] Douglass ridiculed the religious fervor of Reverend Daniel Weeden, who beat a slave woman whom he owned so cruelly that her back was literally raw for weeks. Douglass declared "the religion of the south…a dark shelter under which the darkest, foulest, grossest, and most infernal deeds of slaveholders find the strongest protection."[109]

Still, as womanist theologian Kelly Brown Douglas insists, neither a catalogue of the sins and crimes perpetrated by individual Christians nor a catalogue of the sins and crimes committed by official ecclesial entities and institutions against God's black human creatures explains Christianity's historic and protracted entanglement in their domination.[110] The reasons are multiple, Douglas acknowledges; but her interrogation of Christianity's complicity in chattel slavery and anti-black oppression singles out the toxic mixture of Platonized Christianity, the Enlightenment's stress on reason and rationality, and slavocracy's ideology of white cultural supremacy. These elements bear directly on the preceding analysis of the deconstruction and desacralization of black women's bodies.

The conjunction of religion, rationality, and white supremacy fostered a suspicion, a skepticism about the body and embodiment, which may be teased out of the New Testament. This skepticism accorded outsized primacy to the soul, to reason or rationality, thus solidifying a tendency to distinguish sharply between body and mind, body and soul, flesh and spirit. Although racism as we understand it is a modern phenomenon and unequivocally linked to the Atlantic slave trade of the sixteenth through the nineteenth centuries, assumptions about difference, including skin color, were appropriated and used rhetorically by early Christians to teach and admonish followers as well as to identify dangers to doctrine and devotion: so contends New Testament scholar Gay Byron.[111]

Enlightenment philosophers, including David Hume, Immanuel Kant, and Thomas Jefferson, assumed a correlation between skin color, intellectual limits, ability, and beauty. In the slave market, slave traders, speculators, and slaveholders drew on similar correlations to direct purchase and sale, determine utility, plan breeding, and arrange sexual contact. Some interpretations of Enlightenment philosophy drove these correlations even further, affirming mind over body, thought over matter, and lending a putative ontological status to skin color: White skin and white-skinned people denoted goodness, purity, beauty, abstinence, intelligence, superiority; black skin and black-skinned people denoted evil, impurity, ugliness, hypersexuality, ignorance, inferiority. White skin invested slaveholders with near absolute power in relation to black enslaved people, mocking divine creation and functionally displacing divine authority.

The upshot of this conjunction of skepticism about the body, focus on rationality, and the ideology of white cultural supremacy was the objectification and brutalization of black women's bodies. The technology of the slave market objectified and consumed black bodies, rendering them as skilled parts and packaging them for sale as drudge laborers or breeders, desecrating their bodies and sexuality, souls and spirituality. To reclaim and heal those bodies, to mend the rupture of body and soul, to reconsecrate sexuality required a fundamental grasp of the meaning of bodily integrity and of the power of eros as holy. By making available to black women a life of chastity, of consecrated communal Christian life or protoconventual life in the context of chattel slavery and plaçage, Henriette Delille demonstrated such a grasp. She realized this through choosing to love.

III.

THE SUBVERSIVE
POWER OF LOVE

Enslaved women, Harriet Jacobs stated flatly, were not "allowed to have any pride of character. It is deemed a crime in [them] to wish to be virtuous."[112] Free women of color were not spared the contempt of their person or their virtue. In the Western world, conventual life has always provided women with a "perfectly acceptable social identity outside marriage."[113] Given the deconstruction and commodification of black women's bodies and the exoticization of their sex and sexuality, the choice of this way of life may be read as a bold, critical, even political, strategy for evading sexual abuse, securing and exerting control over of the body, even directing destiny. Perhaps this impulse characterized the refusal of nineteen-year-old Josephine Bakhita when ordered by her Italian slaveholders to leave the convent to which they sent her for religious instruction. Bakhita never fully disclosed what she endured during her capture and enslavement as a young girl-child in the

Sudan. But, those who knew her during her final illness recall not only her nightmares, but also her silence about their content.[114]

Plaçage, as an institutional arrangement, offered a progressive if ambiguous strategy for freedom. On the one hand, free women of color waged their bodies on behalf of the social freedoms and opportunities of their children; on the other hand, they ached as their daughters' bodies and virtue were corrupted, their sons' honor and ambition frustrated. Plaçage was disturbing, drenched in sensuality, and spawned an opaque morality. Perhaps Henriette Delille came to such a conclusion in pondering the life of her sister Cécile or the lives of the women around her or, perhaps, she endured an excruciating personal loss. We do not know. What we do know is that she sought a way out of this murky context—for the sake of her soul, her person, her body. Perhaps she hoped that public ministry in the name of Jesus Christ might serve as a model for others—incarnating the meaning of bodily integrity, of religious, intellectual, and moral self-transcendence. We do not know. What we do know is that she refused to comply with the expectations of her caste, class, and social standing.

The way out of plaçage required that Henriette Delille break decisively with the cultural and religious horizon or worldview within which she was born, brought up, and educated. This could not have been an easy decision to make, but it was surely the result of grasping and choosing a true good. Moreover, such a break signals a shift in her understanding and evaluation of the social milieu in which she lived. So radical a break could not have been provoked by mere survival or escape or fear; such motives could not have provided warrant enough. Black women who aspired to religious life in the nineteenth century faced obstacles from church and society. Their commitment would have had to have been sustained by something far greater and more profound. Theologically, we can say that Henriette Delille's decision was a result of conversion.

"Conversion is basic to Christian living." [115] It is a radical change of course: a woman (man) takes such a decisive, thoroughgoing turn in a new direction that her (or his) entire life's orientation is changed. Growth toward and in this change may be prolonged, even throughout a lifetime, but its processes are disclosed and embodied in a few crucial judgments and decisions. This change is not simply coincident with age or maturity or personal development. Conversion denotes a profound change through which someone new emerges. Lonergan puts it graphically: "It is as if one's eyes were opened and one's former world faded and fell away."[116] And the change that conversion brings about permeates and enriches the cumulative series of developments that are manifest in every area of her (or his) human living.

The break with the former horizon, which Delille made explicit in her judgment and decision to live differently, is what Lonergan refers to as a "vertical exercise of freedom," of self-determination.[117] And in living out the concrete, draining, difficult day-to-day implications of her decision, her exercise in self-determination, Delille embodied the meaning of self-transcendence.

I propose that in order to realize her freedom Henriette Delille chose *to love*: that she experienced an attraction toward divine love that blotted out all else; that she recognized, whether gradually or in a single blinding moment, that the meaning of passion and desire are related ineluctably to divine love, to the absolute love of Christ for concrete human beings, to compassionate active solidarity; that her declaration of love involved a transformation of desire; that her free choice of a countercultural way of life actually and implicitly reconceived, redefined, and reconsecrated the colonized and abused bodies of black women. Such is the subversive power of love.

Passion and Transformation of Desire

In the morally foul atmosphere in which black female bodies were debased, surely Henriette Delille questioned the meanings of passion and desire. All around her women and men claimed to be falling in and out of love, accepted societally determined roles, and involved themselves in commercial transactions that parodied love. Surely she found this disillusioning, tasteless, and offensive. Like all human beings, she yearned to love and to be loved, yearned for genuine passionate encounter. Such longings are normal aspects of human nature and are wholesome and holy. The wisdom of centuries of Christian living teaches that these human longings are met only by the love of God, by union with the divine.

Let us suppose, then, that after an intense religious experience, Henriette Delille turned away from temptation to easy love and easy loves; she fell in love with God. Falling in love with God is "otherworldly falling in love."[118] To fall in love with God is to fall in love with Someone transcendent, Someone who draws us toward self-transcendence, Someone who has a passion for human beings.[119] Henriette Delille responded to this divine passion, this gratuitous love by the free gift of her self—mind, heart, soul, and body "without qualifications, conditions, or reservations."[120] Certainly, her response may be associated with what theologians for centuries have named the "natural desire to see God." Yet, we ought not to discount or dismiss her longing desire, her passion for something more, for Someone. Henriette Delille may never have read Augustine, but she would have resonated with his declaration of love: "O God, you have made us for yourself, and our hearts are restless until they rest in thee."

God's passionate love dismantled and abolished the horizon that heretofore had shaped her concern and interest, drew her ever more deeply into the divine self, opened, expanded, and flooded her heart. God's passionate love transformed not only what she desired, but her very desiring self. Her deepest desires were fulfilled, "for being in love with God [is] the ultimate fulfillment of [our] capacity for self-transcendence."[121] Delille's experience of God's passionate love gave rise to a desire for new and transformed valuing, choosing, acting, and living. We do not know what Henriette Delille experienced, but as John of the Cross tells us, "Once the taste and savor of the spirit is experienced, everything carnal is insipid."[122] What we do know is that she was prompted to write: "I believe in God. I hope in God. I love. I [desire] to live and die for God." These are the words of a person in love with God. They signify what Carmelite Constance FitzGerald describes as "a decisive, preferential choice of the heart for God, a conscious shift in one's focus of meaning which ever so slowly redirects and claims desire."[123]

Being-in-Love

"Being-in-love is a subjectivity transformed."[124] In other words, God's love worked in Henriette Delille a transformation that gave birth to new values, new hope, new possibilities. Perhaps she "experience[d] the inner fire and the inner light…the living flame of love that [made her] being to be *being-in-love*."[125] One way of embodying response to love of God is voluntary consecrated chastity.[126]

The practice of sexual abstinence has deep roots in Judaism and Christianity—Jews for the sake of Torah study, Christians in imitation of Christ.[127] New Testament scholar Sandra Schneiders contends that first- and second-generation Christian women who claimed virginity for explicitly religious reasons were "seen as a dangerous challenge to patriarchal social structures of both family and state."

> Women who declared themselves unavailable as reproductive agents to carry on the family name, seal interfamily alliances, or provide the future citizens of the Empire because they were 'married to Christ' were refusing not only their species role, but also their assigned social role as property of men and state.[128]

As a gesture of personal autonomy and control of the body, virginal commitment may be read as radical, even protofeminist. But, as Schneiders asserts, these women "were in fact giving absolute priority to their own spiritual agenda in the face of overwhelming pressure to the contrary."[129]

Henriette Delille and the free black women who gathered as the Congregation of the Sisters of the

Presentation understood societal and familial pressure to conform to the social norms of their caste and class. Although, in their earliest and informal phase, the women did not declare formal religious vows as the group evolved toward a protoreligious congregation, both Davis and Gould think that the women quite likely took private vows. But even in the group's first phase, Delille prepared directives that counseled members toward "gentleness and prudence," "edifying example," and the avoidance of "serious failings" that could give rise to scandal. Should a member refuse to heed a thrice-repeated "charitable" admonishment, her name was to be removed from the membership register of the Congregation.[130]

Provision for correction would not have been uncalled-for. French-born American-trained priest Michael Portier organized a confraternity of young gens de couleur libres in 1817 to evangelize and instruct the enslaved people. Writing to the rector of the Grande Seminaire in Lyon, Portier boasted of the young people's fervor ("They wear a red ribbon and a cross and they promise to fight daily like valiant soldiers of Jesus Christ") and fidelity "in Babylon, in the midst of scandals."[131]

The quality and power of consecrated chastity as lived by free black women would have had a sharp countercultural impact in the context of slavery and plaçage. The prevailing ideology of slavocracy stigmatized both enslaved and free black women as inherently immoral; at the same time, plaçage was steeped in an ambiguous morality that tainted all involved. Emphasis on avoiding occasions of temptation, on modesty, even on bodily deportment and simplicity in dress would have been common to any society of pious women. In this particular social context, adverting to outward signs of restraint in personal comportment may have been imperative. But consecrated chastity as the reservation of one's person, one's body is neither privation nor concession; rather, it is a form of self-transcendence. Moreover, consecration of the heart, the serious, quiet cultivation of an interior life of prayer, might be of equal if not greater importance.

Being in Love

Love of God forms the ground of human authenticity, of self-transcendence; cognitive, moral, and practical liberation are rooted in this love. Christian witness with its concrete intersubjective and interpersonal dimensions is essential to this love.[132] Christian witness demands an engagement with bodies, not their denial; a struggle with history, not surrender to it. The Sisters of the Presentation sought to live this engagement and struggle in imitation of the first Christians: "Now the whole group of those who believed were of one heart and soul, and no one claimed private ownership of any possessions, but everything they owned was held in

common" (Acts 4:32). The women devoted themselves to care of the infirm and poor, prayer and
praise, instructing others in the faith, sharing all
things in common—constituting themselves as an
ekklesia, an assembly of the baptized.

By 1894, the "little flock" begun as the Sisters of
the Presentation were known as the Sisters of the
Holy Family and deeply embedded in the religious
and cultural fabric of New Orleans. Thirty-two years
earlier, Mère Delille had died relatively unknown,
"except by the poor and the insignificant."[133] Was she
the seed that had fallen into the ground so that it
might give life? In that same year, Sister Mary
Bernard Deggs was asked to write an account of the
early period (1842–1883) of the foundation. Deggs
shapes her memoir around the lives of the earliest
superiors—Delille, Gaudin, Charles, Mother Marie
Magdalene Alpaugh, Mother Marie Cecilia Capla,
and Mother Mary Austin Jones.

Mère Delille left her sisters a legacy of para-
mount service to the enslaved and poor; she committed them as well to the embrace of holy poverty.
Deggs recounted several anecdotes of the sisters'
material privation.

Many were the times that the foundresses had
nothing to eat but cold hominy that had been left
from some rich family's table. It is not necessary
to say a word about their clothing, for it was

more like Joseph's coat that was of many pieces and colors darned, until darn was not the word.[134]

And again:

Many a night did our dear sisters, after working all day, pray that some dear friend would send them a few spoonfuls of sugar. One time a servant came with a silver waiter with what one might call a grand dinner. Others sent us bundles of candles. Others came with a few pounds of coffee and others, if the weather was cold, with a wheelbarrow of wood and of nut coal. Many ladies, knowing how poor we were, often sent us old shoes or boots to wear in the yard when it rained.[135]

Courage also was included in Mère Delille's legacy. Deggs remembered that after emancipation some free people of color, former slaveholders, importuned the sisters to terminate religious instruction to the newly freed people.

[T]hat was asking too much of our sisters, for our dear Lord said, "Go and teach all nations" (Matt 18:19–20). We, as sisters, are more obliged than others to teach all to know their God. And the day that we would refuse would be the day of sin for us, for our dear Lord said in another place that He had not come for the just, but to save sinners (Matt 9:13; Mk 2:17, Lk 5:32). This would have been preaching one thing and practicing another…[136]

But the sisters equivocated, if agonizingly so, when asked by that same class of people to separate their children from the children of emancipated slaves.

Yet, an astonishing example of love's subversive power may be found in another anecdote in which Deggs described the purchase in 1870 of a building for St. Mary's School. During the period of enslavement, this building and its grounds, located on Chartres Street, had served as a trader's slave pen.

> After the late war, many in this city looked on the old house as a disgraceful place and it was abandoned. No one would think of buying it for the very reason that it had previously been a trader's yard and many sins had been committed at that place, not only sins, but the most horrible crimes. It must have been God's will that our sisters should buy this place to expiate the crimes that had been committed there.[137]

Here enslaved black women and men were packaged and displayed, examined and handled, assessed and purchased—their value turning on a calculus of profit and pleasure. Could such a dwelling be capable of exorcism, of redemption?

Expiation calls for remorse, contrition, amendment of purpose and performance, and change of heart. We expect, perhaps even require, those who have committed offenses or done grievous wrong to work out recompense in sincere sorrow, amend behavior, and live concretely into and out of change of heart. What might it mean for Deggs to link the purchase of this property by the Sisters of the Holy Family to the idea that God wills black women to expiate the heinous sins committed against black women (and men)?

Chattel slavery, the war that contributed to its demise, its discriminatory aftermath, and plaçage comprise at least two centuries of maldistributed, transgenerational, negative, massive suffering for black women and men.[138] These cruel and public events brought black and white, female and male, religion and culture, economy and policy face to face with a situation that defies human imagination and calls for uncommon religious, intellectual, and moral resources. Such congealed evil in society may be understood as "societal impasse."[139] Societal impasse calls for as much remorse and repentance, healing and creativity, mercy and justice as we human beings can muster. Perhaps even more was required of the daughters of Mère Delille. "This is my commandment, that you love one another as I have loved you" (John 15:12).

Love your enemies, do good to those who hate you, bless those who curse you, pray for those who abuse you...If you love those who love you, what credit is that to you? For even sinners love those who love them...Your reward will be great, and you will be children of the Most High; for he

61

is kind to the ungrateful and the wicked. Be merciful, just as your Father is merciful. (Luke 6:27–28, 32, 35b–36)

Delille left her daughters a legacy of love—love, powerful and subversive; love that is self-transcending; love that brings good out of the injury of evil.

Love is patient; love is kind; love is not envious or boastful or arrogant or rude. It does not insist on its own way; it is not irritable or resentful; it does not rejoice in wrongdoing, but rejoices in the truth. It bears all things, believes all things, hopes all things, endures all things. Love never ends. (1 Cor 13:4–8a)

To the pain and problem of evil, to societal impasse such love poses a transcendent solution, and that solution is patterned in the passion, death, and resurrection of Jesus of Nazareth who is the Christ of God. Such love absorbs the unintelligibility, the irrationality of the sin of enslavement—objectification, physical assault, sexual exploitation, manipulation, and psychic battering of human beings. Such love meets evil with good, breaks the cycle of violence and oppression. In order to meet evil with good and with love calls for living into and out of divine grace gratuitously offered; calls for openness and cooperation with that grace in personal, psychic, intelligent, moral, intersubjective, and religious development; calls for drawing the supernatural resources of faith, hope, and charity.[140]

Thus, love and prayer as active cooperation with divine grace might hallow the ground where black women had been forced to endure the pornographic gaze of sellers and buyers of human flesh. Love and prayer as cooperation with divine grace might purify the place where black women had been handled, assaulted, and raped. Love and prayer for enslaved women (and men), love and prayer for those who sold, bought, forced, and violated them.

Was love and prayer effective, fruitful? From this dreadful site, Deggs tells us, came "one of the most successful houses that the Holy Family Sisters ever had since its foundation."[141]

CONCLUSION

"I believe in God. I hope in God. I love. I [desire] to live and die for God." With this resolution, Henriette Delille embarked on the journey of a lifetime, a journey rooted in eschatological hope. The cause for her canonization presses forward; surely she may be counted among the "friends of God and prophets."[142]

Mère Delille's earliest ministry was serving as godparent for baptisms or a witness to marriages. This gesture may not seem to carry countercultural weight, but she focused her attention and concern on enslaved and free black people. It may not have been an easy matter for these women and men to locate sponsors or witnesses. Matrimony between free black and enslaved people required the permission of the slaveholder. Marriages between free black people and foreign (French) nationals were prohibited by civil law. By putting herself forward to act as a witness in such instances, was she opposing concubinage?[143] Her ministerial commitment and life choice suggest that she was. Does her service as a frequent witness to a marriage, a sacrament intimately associated with the body, sex, and sexuality, signal regard for body and soul, for the humanness of enslaved people, whose humanity was suspect? Her ministerial commitment and life choice suggest that she was.

The Sisters of the Presentation struggled; so did the early members of the Sisters of the Holy Family. On more than one occasion women left and returned to their families or went abroad. But Mère Delille clung to a vision of something new, something never before dared. Davis concludes: "She seemed to have had the vision and singleness of purpose to bind the others in unity and to join them all in common responsibility."[144]

When Henriette Delille stepped outside the system of plaçage, she did so publicly and waged her body for the freedom of the body of Christ. She refused to be acted upon by male and female others, to allow them to seal her fate. She took control of her body, its situatedness in time and place and circumstance. That body functioned as a text on which she inscribed with authority her own vision of new life and love. She wrote herself vividly into the Communion of Saints.

When Henriette Delille transgressed the conventional expectations of her caste, social class, and gender, she did so publicly and publicly reclaimed not only her own body, but symbolically wrested the bodies of enslaved and other free women of color from sexual coercion. Her reclaimed body signified the struggle to love and to become authentically human in the face of a brutal and brutalizing world.

When Henriette Delille defied the tepid Catholicism of her day, she did so publicly and sought a new way of being in public ministry with eschatological and situated hope. Rather than submit to ecclesiastical indifference, Delille exercised her intelligence, creativity, and moral agency in a preferential option for despised enslaved blacks, the poor, aged, and infirm. Indeed, her ministry and that of her sisters followed the path that took Jesus of Nazareth to the outcast, marginalized, and poor. Henriette Delille situated herself and her ministry among "her people"—not only acting for them, but also being with and among them; not only doing them good, but also sharing in their privation, discrimination, and suffering. She lived out concretely a love that subverted color, caste, and circumstance in order to live in imitation of Jesus.

"I believe in God. I hope in God. I love. I [desire] to live and die for God." These words shape the arc of Henriette Delille's destiny. Cyprian Davis rightly insists that these words "express more than a pious sentiment."[145] Indeed, they signify the text that is her bodily lived life. Davis calls her elusive, but her bodily citations are enfleshed in generations of spiritual daughters. In her struggle to live and die for God, Henriette Delille defied social convention and cultural custom, rejected the tepid religiosity of so many, and incarnated extraordinary moral audacity and spiritual courage through the subversive power of love.

NOTES

1. For the dating of the daguerreotype, see Sister Mary Bernard Deggs, *No Cross, No Crown: Black Nuns in Nineteenth-Century New Orleans*, ed. Virginia Meacham Gould and Charles E. Nolan (Bloomington & Indianapolis: Indiana University Press, 2001), n.p.

2. Bernard Lonergan, *Method in Theology* (New York: Herder & Herder, 1972), 112.

3. Cyprian Davis, *Henriette Delille, Servant of Slaves, Witness to the Poor* (New Orleans: Archdiocese of New Orleans/Sisters of the Holy Family, 2004), 35.

4. Davis, *The History of Black Catholics in the United States* (New York: Crossroad Publishing, 1990), 98.

5. Ibid., 99–100; Thaddeus John Posey, "An Unwanted Commitment: The Spirituality of the Early Oblate Sisters of Providence, 1829–1890," Ph.D. diss. St. Louis University, 1993; idem, "Praying in the Shadows: The Oblate Sisters of Providence, A Look at Nineteenth-Century Black Spirituality," *U.S. Catholic Historian* 12, no. 1 (Winter 1994): 11–30; Diane Batts Morrow, *Persons of Color and Religious at the Same Time: The Oblate Sisters of Providence, 1828–1860* (Chapel Hill, NC: University of North Carolina Press, 2002).

6. Kimberly S. Hanger, *Bounded Lives, Bounded Places* (Durham & London: Duke University Press, 1997), 17–54.

7. In *Cane River* (New York: Warner Books, Inc., 2001), Lalita Tademy relates the story of her enslaved female ancestors, who experienced forced as well as consensual sexual relations with white men, who were planters and well-to-do entrepreneurs, in rural Louisiana. Tademy presses sound historical research and extensive oral interviews through vivid fiction to capture the resolute courage of these women in negotiating education, financial support, and property for their offspring as well as in navigating the class and color barriers among whites, enslaved blacks, and free people of color. Other novels dealing with the sexual exploitation of black women under enslavement and colonialism include Austin Clarke, *The Polished Hoe* (Toronto: Thomas Allen Publishers, 2002); and Anne Rice, *Feast of All Saints* (New York: Ballantine Books, 1980) for a novel about the free people of color.

8. Davis, *Henriette Delille, Servant of Slaves, Witness to the Poor,* 8.

9. Deborah Gray White, *Ar'n't I a Woman? Female Slaves in the Plantation South* rev. ed (New York: W. W. Norton & Company, 1999), 27.

10. Mary Ann Hinsdale, *Women Shaping Theology, 2004 Madeleva Lecture in Spirituality* (New York/Mahwah, NJ: Paulist Press, 2006).

11. For one of the major collections see George P. Rawick, ed., *The American Slave: A Composite Autobiography* 19 vols. (1941; Westport, CT: Greenwood Publishing Company, 1972). For some interpretative

studies of slave narratives see Marion Wilson Starling, *The Slave's Narrative* (Washington, DC: Howard University Press, 1981); Charles T. Davis and Henry Louis Gates, Jr., *The Slave's Narrative* (New York: Oxford University Press, 1984). For studies of black women's narrative traditions see Mary Helen Washington, "Meditations on History: The Slave Woman's Voice," in her edited *Invented Lives: Narratives of Black Women, 1860–1960* (Garden City, NY: Anchor Press/Doubleday & Company, Inc., 1987); Joanne M. Braxton, *Black Women Writing Autobiography: A Tradition Within a Tradition* (Philadelphia: Temple University Press, 1988).

12. For some studies of black women's sexual oppression under chattel slavery, see my "'Wading Through Many Sorrows': Towards a Theology of Suffering in Womanist Perspective" in Emilie M. Townes, ed., *A Troubling in My Soul: Womanist Reflections on Evil and Suffering* (Maryknoll, NY: Orbis Books, 1993), 109–29; Catherine Clinton and Michele Gillespie, eds., *The Devil's Lane: Sex and Race in the Early South* (New York & London: Oxford University Press, 1997); Hélène Lecaudey, "Behind the Mask: Ex-Slave Women and Interracial Sexual Relations," in Patricia Morton, ed., *Discovering the Women in Slavery: Emancipating Perspectives* (Athens & London: The University of Georgia Press, 1996), 260–77.

13. Jerah Johnson, "Colonial New Orleans: A Fragment of the Eighteenth-Century French Ethos," in Arnold R. Hirsch and Joseph Logsdon, eds., *Creole New Orleans: Race and Americanization* (Baton Rouge: Louisiana State University Press, 1992), 32, 33.

14. Ibid., 45.

15. Gwendolyn Midlo Hall, "The Formation of Afro-Creole Culture," in *Creole New Orleans*, 58.

16. Emily Clark and Virginia Meacham Gould, "The Feminine Face of Afro-Catholicism in New Orleans, 1727–1852," *The William and Mary Quarterly* April 2002 http://www.historycooperative.org/cgi-bin/justtopcgi?act=justtop&url=http://www.historycooperative.org/journals/wm/59.2/clark.html (29 Nov. 2005), par 9.

17. In July 2005, as a member of the faculty of the Institute for Black Catholic Studies, Xavier University of Louisiana, New Orleans, I participated with colleagues and students in the Commemoration of the *Maafa*, sponsored annually by the Ashé Cultural Center of New Orleans. *Maafa*, a Kiswahili word, denotes great disaster; it is used to refer to the Middle Passage. The processional route from Congo Square in Louis Armstrong Park to the Mississippi River took us past a former "Slave exchange," where we paused to offer libation and to pray. See Walter Johnson, *Soul by Soul* (Cambridge, MA: Harvard University Press, 1999), illustrations 9, 10.

18. John England, "Letters to the Honorable John Forsyth on the Subject of Domestic Slavery," in *The Works of the Right Reverend John England* (Baltimore: John Murphy, 1849), 3: 112, cited in Davis, *The History of Black Catholics in the United States*, 39–40; see Joel Panzer, "The Popes and Slavery," *The Dunwoodie Review*, vol. 18 (1995): 78–109.

19. Randall M. Miller, "Catholics in a Protestant World: The Old South Example," in Samuel H. Hill, ed., *Varieties of Southern Religious Experience* (Baton Rouge, LA: Louisiana State University Press, 1988),

115; see also Davis, *The History of Black Catholics in the United States*, 35–41.

20. Miller, "Catholics in a Protestant World: The Old South Example," in *Varieties of Southern Religious Experience*, 121.

21. Jon L. Wakelyn, "Catholic Elites in the Slaveholding South," in Randall M. Miller and Jon L. Wakelyn, eds., *Catholics in the Old South: Essays on Church and Culture* (Macon, GA: Mercer University Press, 1983), 211–39.

22. Davis, *The History of Black Catholics in the United States*, 35–39; R. Emmett Curran, "'Splendid Poverty': Jesuit Slaveholding in Maryland, 1805–1838," in *Catholics in the Old South*, 125–46.

23. Francis Maxwell, *Slavery and the Catholic Church* (Westminster, MD: Christian Classics, 1975) 10–12.

24. John Peter Marschall, "Francis Patrick Kenrick, 1851–1863: The Baltimore Years," Ph.D. diss., The Catholic University of America, 1965, 332, cited in Richard R. Duncan, "Catholics and the Church in the Antebellum Upper South," in *Catholics in the Old South*, 76.

25. Davis, *Henriette Delille, Servant of Slaves, Witness to the Poor*, 73–75.

26. Auguste Martin was the first bishop of Louisiana (1803–1875), Augustin Verot bishop of St. Augustine in Florida (1804–1876), and John England bishop of South Carolina (1786–1842).

27. Maria Caravaglios, "A Roman Critique of Pro-Slavery Views of Bishop Martin of Natchitoches, Louisiana," *Records of the American Catholic His-*

torical Society of Philadelphia 83 (1972): 51, cited in Davis, *Henriette Delille, Servant of Slaves, Witness to the Poor*, 73.

28. Davis, *Henriette Delille, Servant of Slaves, Witness to the Poor*, 73–75; see also Miller, "The Failed Mission: The Catholic Church and Black Catholics in the Old South," in *Catholics in the Old South*, 149–70; Edward J. Misch, "The American Bishops and the Negro from the Civil War to the Third Plenary Council of Baltimore: 1865–1884," Ph.D. diss., Pontifical Gregorian University, Rome, 1968; Jamie T. Phelps, "The Mission Ecclesiology of John R. Slattery: A Study of an African American Mission of the Catholic Church in the Nineteenth Century," Ph.D. diss., The Catholic University of America, 1989, especially 1–146.

29. Miller, "Catholics in a Protestant World: The Old South Example," in *Varieties of Southern Religious Experience*, 121, 127–128.

30. Gould and Nichols, "Introduction," *No Cross, No Crown*, xxv.

31. Exploring the French Revolution: Liberty, Equality, Fraternity, "The *Code Noir* (The Black Code)," http://chnm.gmu.edu/revolution/d/335/ (14 April 2007).

32. The first article of the *Code* expelled all Jews from the colonies "at the risk of confiscation of their persons and their goods" (art. I). In the Dutch colonies in the Caribbean, Jews participated in the slave trading and slaveholding, but in French colonies they were not allowed to own property or slaves.

33. The *Code Noir*, art. 2–4, 6–7, 9, 12, 15–16, 19, 28, 31; Davis, *Henriette Delille, Servant of Slaves, Witness to the Poor*, 86–87.

34.   Kimberly S. Hanger, "'The Fortunes of Women in America': Spanish New Orleans's Free Women of African Descent and their Relations with Slave Women," in *Discovering the Women in Slavery*, 157; idem, *Bounded Lives, Bounded Places*, 34–51; Robin Blackburn, *The Making of New World Slavery: From the Baroque to the Modern, 1492–1800* (London: Verso, 1997), 51.

35.   George Reid Andrews, *Afro-Latin America, 1800–2000* (Oxford: Oxford University Press, 2004), 33–34.

36.   Harriet Jacobs, *Incidents in the Life of a Slave Girl*, ed. L. Maria Child (New York: Harcourt Brace Jovanovich, Publishers, 1973), 15, 25.

37.   Wilma King, "Out of Bounds: Emancipated and Enslaved Women in Antebellum America," in David Barry Gaspar and Darlene Clark Hine, eds., *Beyond Bondage: Free Women of Color in the Americas* (Urbana and Chicago: University of Illinois Press, 2004), 129–30.

38.   Gould, "Henriette Delille, Free Women of Color, and Catholicism in Antebellum New Orleans, 1727–1852," in *Beyond Bondage*, 272 (italics mine).

39.   Peter Kolchin, *American Slavery, 1619–1877* (New York: Hill & Wang, 1993), 82–83. The term Creole derives from the Spanish criollo, the Portuguese crioulo. For an historical and sociocultural analysis of the term, see Joseph G. Tregle, "Creoles and Americans," in *Creole New Orleans*, 131–85.

40.   King, "Out of Bounds: Emancipated and Enslaved Women in Antebellum America," in *Beyond Bondage*, 132.

41.   Davis, *Henriette Delille, Servant of Slaves, Witness to the Poor*, 88; Gould, "'If I Can't Have My

Rights, I Can Have My Pleasures, and if They Won't Give Me Wages, I Can Take Them': Gender and Slave Labor in Antebellum New Orleans," in *Discovering the Women in Slavery*, 179–201.

42. Loren Schweninger, "The Fragile Nature of Freedom: Free Women of Color in the U. S. South," in *Beyond Bondage*, 107.

43. Davis, *Henriette Delille, Servant of Slaves, Witness to the Poor*, x.

44. David Walker, *Appeal to the Coloured Citizens of the World*, ed. Peter P. Hinks (1829; University Park, PA: Pennsylvania State University Press, 2000); Maria W. Stewart, *America's First Black Woman Political Writer: Essays and Speeches*, ed. with an Introduction by Marilyn Richardson (1840; Bloomington, IN: Indiana University Press, 1987); Frederick Douglass, *The Narrative and Selected Writings*, ed. Michael Meyer (New York: Modern Library/Random House, 1984).

45. Davis, *Henriette Delille, Servant of Slaves, Witness to the Poor*, 2–3, 98–99; Gould, "Henriette Delille, Free Women of Color, and Catholicism in Antebellum New Orleans, 1727–1852," in *Beyond Bondage*, 273.

46. Gould, "Henriette Delille, Free Women of Color, and Catholicism in Antebellum New Orleans, 1727–1852," in *Beyond Bondage*, 274.

47. Davis, *Henriette Delille, Servant of Slaves, Witness to the Poor*, 15–16.

48. Marie Josephe was also known as Josephine. In *Henriette Delille, Servant of Slaves, Witness to the Poor*, Davis conjectures that her father may have been Antonio Diaz or Dias, 5–9, 98.

49. Deggs, *No Cross, No Crown*, 10; Gould and Nichols, "Introduction," *No Cross, No Crown*, xxx.

50. Gould and Nichols, "Introduction," *No Cross, No Crown*, xxx; Davis, *Henriette Delille, Servant of Slaves, Witness to the Poor*, 22; Sister Frances Jerome Woods, "Congregations of Religious Women in the Old South," in *Catholics in the Old South*, 115.

51. Davis, *Henriette Delille, Servant of Slaves, Witness to the Poor*, 30.

52. Ibid., 36.

53. Ibid., 35.

54. Ibid., 46.

55. Facsimile of "The Rules and Regulations for the Congregation of the Sisters of the Presentation of the Blessed Virgin Mary under the Invocation of Mary the Virgin of the Holy Presentation. Founded in New Orleans the 21st November 1836." The French original is in the Archives of the Sisters of the Holy Family, New Orleans, Louisiana.

56. Ibid.

57. Davis, *Henriette Delille, Servant of Slaves, Witness to the Poor*, 40.

58. Ibid., 46–47.

59. Ibid., 41; Gould, "Henriette Delille, Free Women of Color, and Catholicism in Antebellum New Orleans, 1727–1852," in *Beyond Bondage*, 276.

60. Davis, *Henriette Delille, Servant of Slaves, Witness to the Poor*, 59.

61. Clark and Gould, par 59–61; Davis, *Henriette Delille, Servant of Slaves, Witness to the Poor*, 63.

62. Clark and Gould, par 61.

63. Davis, *Henriette Delille, Servant of Slaves, Witness to the Poor*, 15, 64–68.

64. Loren Schweninger, "The Fragile Nature of Freedom: Free Women of Color in the United States," in *Beyond Bondage*, 106.

65. U.S. Constitution, art. 4, sec 2, cl. 2: "No person held to service or labor in one state, under the laws thereof, escaping into another, shall, in consequence of any law or regulation therein, be discharged from such service or labor, but shall be delivered up on claim of the party to whom such service or labor may be due." The Fugitive Slave Law was rooted in this provision and forced Northern involvement in slave trading.

66. The American Colonization Society (ACS) was organized in 1816 by Reverend Robert Finley to remove free blacks and emancipated slaves from the United States. After much negotiation and a failed attempt, in 1821 the ACS established Liberia as a place of return and transported several hundred blacks there. The majority of black people rejected this solution. In "Catholic Elites in the Slaveholding South," Wakelyn calls attention to the endorsement and participation at various times in these schemes by prominent Catholics like Charles Carroll and William Gaston, in *Catholics in the Old South*, 238.

67. Davis, *Henriette Delille, Servant of Slaves, Witness to the Poor*, 15.

68. Wilma King, "Emancipated and Enslaved Women in Antebellum America," in *Beyond Bondage*, 133.

69. *Le Propagateur Catholique. Journal Officiel du diocese de la Nouvelle Orleans*, November 22, 1862,

cited in Davis, *Henriette Delille, Servant of Slaves, Witness to the Poor,* 1.

70. Clark and Gould, par 61.

71. Stephanie M. H. Camp, *Closer to Freedom: Enslaved Women and Everyday Resistance in the Plantation South* (Chapel Hill and London: University of North Carolina Press, 2004), 62.

72. Ibid., 63.

73. Ibid.

74. Walter Johnson, *Soul by Soul* (Cambridge, MA: Harvard University Press, 1999), 138.

75. Ibid., 150–51; see Norman R. Yetman, ed., *When I Was a Slave: Memoirs from the Slave Narrative Collection* (Mineola, NY: Dover Publications, Inc., 2002), 137–38.

76. Solomon Northup, *Twelve Years a Slave* (1853; Mineola, NY: Dover Publications, Inc., 1970), 80.

77. Johnson, *Soul by Soul,* 118, 120.

78. William Wells Brown, *From Fugitive Slave to Free Man: The Autobiographies of William Wells Brown* (1847; Columbia, MO & London: University of Missouri Press, 1993), 43.

79. Johnson, *Soul by Soul,* 138.

80. Yetman, ed., *When I Was a Slave,* 90.

81. James Roberts, *The Narrative of James Roberts: Soldier in the Revolutionary War and the Battle of New Orleans* (Hattiesburg, MS: The Book Farm, 1945), 26.

82. Yetman, ed., *When I Was a Slave,* 148. ["Woman, I'se pay big money for you'se, and I'se done dat for de cause I'se wants you'se to raise me chilluns. I'se put you'se to live with Rufus for dat purpose. Now, if

you'se don't want to be whipped at the stake, you'se do what I'se want."]

83. Brown, *From Fugitive Slave to Free Man*, 70.

84. Yetman, ed., *When I Was a Slave*, 20.

85. Johnson, *Soul by Soul*, 149.

86. Brown, *From Fugitive Slave to Free Man*, 45–46; Melton A. McClaurin, *Celia, a Slave* (Athens, GA: University of Georgia Press, 1991); Carolyn J. Powell, "In Remembrance of Mira: Reflections on the Death of a Slave Woman," in *Discovering the Women in Slavery*, 47–60; Patricia J. Williams, "On Being the Object of Property," *Signs: Journal of Women in Culture and Society* 14, no. 1 (1988): 5–24.

87. Yetman, ed., *Voices from Slavery* (New York: Holt, Rinehart and Winston, 1970), 299. ["Old Massa done so much wrongness I couldn't tell you all of it. Slave girl Betty Lilly always had good clothes and all the privileges. She was a favorite of his'n. But cain't tell all! God's got all."]

88. Ibid., 108. ["Us niggers knowed the doctor took a black woman quick as he did a white and took any on his place he wanted, and he took them often."]

89. Northup, *Twelve Years a Slave*, 50–51.

90. Ibid., 86–87.

91. Johnson, *Soul by Soul*, 113; see also Edward Baptist, "'Cuffy,' 'Fancy Maids,' and 'One-Eyed Men': Rape, Commodification, and the Domestic Slave Trade in the United States," *American Historical Review* 106, no. 5 (December 2001): 1619–50.

92. Jacobs, *Incidents in the Life of a Slave Girl*, 79.

93. Ibid., 53.

94. Ibid., 62, 81.

95. Johnson, *Soul by Soul*, 114.

96. Jacobs, *Incidents in the Life of a Slave Girl*, 34.

97. Cited in Gerder Lerner, ed., *Black Women in White America: A Documentary History* (New York: Vintage Books, 1973), 51–52.

98. Belinda Hurmence, ed., *Before Freedom, When I Just Can Remember: Twenty-seven Oral Histories of Former South Carolina Slaves* (Winston-Salem, NC: John F. Blair, Publisher, 1989), 134.

99. Yetman, ed., *When I Was a Slave,* 108.

100. Barbara Welter, "The Cult of True Womanhood, 1820–1860," in idem, *Dimity Convictions: The American Woman in the Nineteenth Century* (Columbus: University of Ohio Press, 1976), 21–41, cited in Hazel V. Carby, *Reconstructing Womanhood: The Emergence of the Afro-American Woman Novelist* (New York & Oxford: Oxford University Press, 1987), 23.

101. Jacobs, *Incidents in the Life of a Slave Girl,* 27.

102. Johnson, *Soul by Soul*, 112; Delores S. Williams, *Sisters in the Wilderness: The Challenge of Womanist God-Talk* (Maryknoll: Orbis Books, 1993), 62–71.

103. Nell Irvin Painter, "Soul Murder and Slavery: Toward a Fully-Loaded Cost Accounting," in Linda K. Kerber, Alice Kessler Harris, and Kathryn Kish Sklar, eds., *U.S. History as Women's History: New Feminist Essays* (Chapel Hill: University of North Carolina Press, 1995), 125–46, cited in Johnson, *Soul by Soul*, 64.

104. Katie G. Cannon, *Black Womanist Ethics* (Atlanta, GA: Scholars Press, 1989), 40.

105. For excellent theological analyses, see Kelly Brown Douglas, *Sexuality and the Black Church: A Womanist Perspective* (Maryknoll: Orbis Books, 1999);

Anthony B. Pinn and Dwight N. Hopkins, eds., *Loving the Body: Black Religious Studies and the Erotic* (New York: Palgrave Macmillan, 2004); Dwight N. Hopkins, *Being Human: Race, Culture, and Religion* (Minneapolis: Fortress Press, 2005); Emilie M. Townes, *Womanist Ethics and the Cultural Production of Evil* (New York: Palgrave Macmillan, 2006).

106. Miller, "Catholics in a Protestant World: The Old South Example," in *Varieties of Southern Religious Experience*, 121.

107. Ibid., 125–26.

108. Jacobs, *Incidents in the Life of a Slave Girl*, 72.

109. Douglass, *The Narrative*, 85, 86.

110. Kelly Brown Douglas, *What's Faith Got to Do with It? Black Bodies/Christian Souls* (Maryknoll: Orbis Books, 2005), 119–33.

111. Gay L. Byron, *Symbolic Blackness and Ethnic Difference in Early Christian Literature* (London & New York: Routledge, 2002), 123.

112. Jacobs, *Incidents in the Life of a Slave Girl*, 29.

113. Silvia Evangelisti, *Nuns: A History of Convent Life, 1450–1700* (Oxford: Oxford University Press, 2007), 4.

114. Josephine Bakhita was born in 1869 in the Sudan and died as a Canosian Sister of Charity in Schio (Vicenza), Italy in 1947. She was canonized a saint of the Roman Catholic Church on October 1, 2000 by Pope John Paul II. See *Bakhita: From Slavery to Sanctity* (Nairobi: Paulines Publications of Africa, 1993), 4–5, 42–43.

115. Lonergan, *Method in Theology*, 130.

116. Ibid.

117. Ibid., 240.

118. Ibid.

119. Rosemary Haughton, *The Passionate God* (New York/Ramsey: Paulist Press, 1981).

120. Lonergan, *Method in Theology*, 109.

121. Ibid., 106, 111.

122. John of the Cross, *The Collected Works of St. John of the Cross*, rev. ed., trans. Kiernan Kavanaugh and Otilio Rodriguez (Washington, DC: ICS Publications, 1991), The Ascent of Mount Carmel, Book Two, ch. 17, no. 5, 207.

123. Constance FitzGerald, "Transformation in Wisdom: The Subjective Character and Educative Power of Sophia in Contemplation," in Kevin Culligan and Regis Jordan, eds., *Carmel and Contemplation: Transforming Human Consciousness* (Washington, DC: ICS Publications, 2000), 290–91.

124. Kathleen Margaret Williams, "Lonergan and the Transforming Immanence of The Transcendent: Towards a Theology of Grace as the Dynamic State of Being-in-Love with God," D. Theol. diss., Melbourne College of Divinity, 1998, 154.

125. William Johnston, *Mystical Theology: The Science of Love* (London: Harper Collins, 1995), 255.

126. Sandra M. Schneiders in her *Religious Life in a New Millennium*, vol. 2, *Selling All: Commitment, Consecrated Celibacy, and Community in Catholic Religious Life* (New York/Mahwah, NJ: Paulist Press, 2001) distinguishes virginity, chastity, and consecrated celibacy. Here I use the term *chastity*, as it seems more appropriate to nineteenth-century consecrated religious life.

127. See Josephine Massingberd Ford, *A Trilogy on Wisdom and Celibacy* (Notre Dame, IN: University of Notre Dame Press, 1967); Peter Brown, *The Body and Society, Men, Women, and Sexual Renunciation in Early Christianity* (New York: Columbia University Press, 1988).

128. Schneiders, *Selling All: Commitment, Consecrated Celibacy, and Community in Catholic Religious Life*, 182.

129. Ibid., 183.

130. Facsimile of the "Rules and Regulations for the Congregation of the Sisters of the Presentation of the Blessed Virgin Mary."

131. Gould and Nolan, "Introduction," *No Cross, No Crown*, xxxi; Davis, *Henriette Delille: Servant of Slaves, Witness to the Poor*, 21.

132. Lonergan, *Method in Theology*, 327.

133. Davis, *Henriette Delille: Servant of Slaves, Witness to the Poor*, 78.

134. Deggs, *No Cross, No Crown*, 9.

135. Ibid., 9–10.

136. Ibid., 12.

137. Ibid., 46.

138. William R. Jones, *Is God a White Racist?: A Preamble to Black Theology* (Garden City, NY: Anchor Press/Doubleday, 1973), 21–22.

139. FitzGerald, "Impasse and Dark Night," in Joann Wolski Conn, ed., *Women's Spirituality: Resources for Christian Development* (New York/Mahwah, NJ: Paulist Press, 1986), 299.

140. Lonergan, *Insight: A Study of Human Understanding* (New York: Philosophical Library, 1957), 699, 721–23.

141. Deggs, *No Cross, No Crown*, 46.

142. Elizabeth A. Johnson, *Friends of God and Prophets: A Feminist Theological Reading of the Communion of Saints* (New York: Continuum, 1998).

143. Davis, *Henriette Delille, Servant of Slaves, Witness to the Poor*, 41.

144. Ibid., 78.

145. Ibid., 36.

The Madeleva Lecture in Spirituality

This series, sponsored by the Center for Spirituality, Saint Mary's College, Notre Dame, Indiana, honors annually the woman who as president of the college inaugurated its pioneering graduate program in theology, Sister M. Madeleva, C.S.C.

1985
Monika K. Hellwig
Christian Women in a Troubled World

1986
Sandra M. Schneiders
Women and the Word

1987
Mary Collins
Women at Prayer

1988
Maria Harris
Women and Teaching

1989
Elizabeth Dreyer
Passionate Women: Two Medieval Mystics

1990
Joan Chittister, OSB
Job's Daughters

1991
Dolores R. Leckey
Women and Creativity

1992
Lisa Sowle Cahill
Women and Sexuality

1993
Elizabeth A. Johnson
Women, Earth, and Creator Spirit

1994
Gail Porter Mandell
Madeleva: One Woman's Life

1995
Diana L. Hayes
Hagar's Daughters

1996
Jeanette Rodriguez
Stories We Live
Cuentos Que Vivimos

1997
Mary C. Boys
Jewish-Christian Dialogue

1998
Kathleen Norris
The Quotidian Mysteries

1999
Denise Lardner Carmody
An Ideal Church: A Meditation

2000
Sandra M. Schneiders
With Oil in Their Lamps

2001
Mary Catherine Hilkert
Speaking with Authority

2002
Margaret A. Farley
Compassionate Respect

2003
Sidney Callahan
Women Who Hear Voices

2004
Mary Ann Hinsdale, IHM
Women Shaping Theology

[No Lecture in 2005]

2006
Susan A. Ross
For the Beauty of the Earth

2008
Barbara Fiand
Awe-Filled Wonder